THE EVERYTHING GREEN handbook 2011

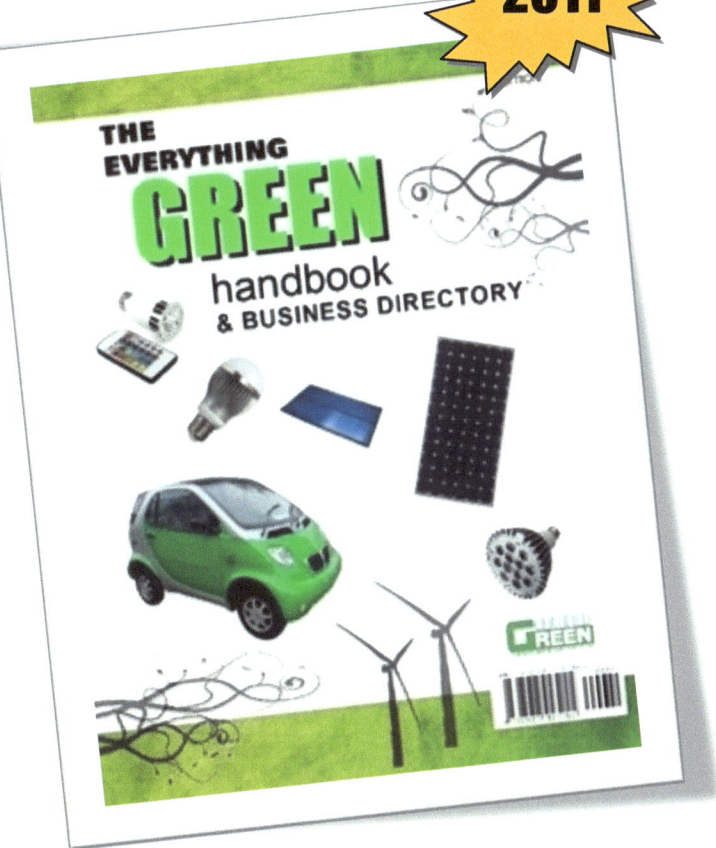

PUBLISHED BY
Austin Livingston
P.O. Box 5660
Salton City, CA 92275

Graphics: Blue Waters Media Group

Editor: Lucena Buffington

All of us at Green Direct USA are focused on providing you informative, fun and useful information to help you on your journey to "Going Green".

If you have any questions, suggestions, comments or products you would like us to feature in our next printing please write us at:

D. Austin Livingston
P.O. Box 5660
Salton City, CA 92275

Third Edition January 2011

THE EVERYTHING GREEN HANDBOOK
by D. Austin Livingston

Copyright © 2006-2011 D. Austin Livingston
All Rights Reserved.
Printed in the United States of America.

ISBN: 978-0-557-84154-7

HOW GREEN ARE YOU?

So what's all the buzz about "going green"? Ultimately, the benefit is that open-minded acceptance of proven "green technologies" will bring investment, training, jobs and prosperity to the communities that adopt them. The end result is a renewed appreciation for our environment and managed energy costs for those that live and work in these communities. Most importantly, security for future generations that will be grateful for our vision and selflessness.

Long-term economic growth is the fruit that's harvested when we plant the seeds of green initiatives today. Going Green is much more than a passing fad, it's a lifestyle that encourages every member of society to take a stand and get involved. The Everything Green Handbook and Business Directory is designed to be a resource tool to help you explore and dive into the future of Green Technology. Turn the pages, scribble notes, visit the businesses and websites, and begin your own journey. Don't forget to take lots of pictures and let us know just how you're "greening" your Home, Office or Community. We'd love to hear from you.

D. Austin Livingston

THE EVERYTHING GREEN HANDBOOK - CONTENTS

- How Green Are You   5
- Pathways To Synergy Building Blocks   8
- Building Systems   10
- Green Home Profile   11
- Pathways To Synergy Solutions   12
- Solar Power Is On The Move   17
- Solar Energy Showcase   18
- Wind Energy Showcase   20
- EV Showcase   22
- Jobs, Training & Prosperity   23
- Green Scenes, Ideas & Solutions   26
- LED Lighting   27
- Green Products Profiles   28

The Everything Green Handbook

HOW GREEN ARE YOU?

There are as many definitions of "green" as there are shades of color. Wikipedia defines a green building, also known as a sustainable building as " a structure that is designed, built, renovated, operated, or reused in an ecological and resource-efficient manner."

Dade County Florida's Website reads that, "Sustainable building practices go beyond energy and water conservation to incorporate environmentally sensitive site planning, resource efficient building materials and superior indoor environmental quality." The website lists five key benefits of sustainable construction that seems to concisely capture the "spirit" of the green building concept.

- Lower electric and water utility costs
- Effective use of building materials
- Enhanced health and productivity
- Long-term economic returns
- Reduced environmental impact

The need to reduce costs associated with energy production and importing building materials, the importance of conserving water and natural resources and minimizing environmental impact are challenges that are even more paramount within our island communities. Green initiatives provide excellent benefits but carry a price tag associated with implementation. We've looked at the benefits and the challenges, but what are the affordable solutions?

Lower Electric Costs

Thin-film Solar and Atmospheric Water Generation are two affordable technologies that fit exceptionally well in the Caribbean region for example. With the abundance of sunshine received intermingled with overcast days, it is still estimated that a solar radiation of 4-5 hours per day is typical for the region. Using lightweight thin-film solar, with a capacity of an estimated 5 watts/sq ft. a typical 1,200 sq ft home could easily support a roof laminated 3,000 Watt solar power system. A system of this size would generate an estimated 12-15kWh per day. By reducing electrical lighting, cooling, and appliance loads to less than 4k the solar system can also be reduced in size.

How do we reduce our electrical load calculations? Design and retrofit with L.E.D. Lighting is one simple solution. A typical home using high efficiency L.E.D. lighting would use just under 250 Watts for the entire lighting circuit and provide equal or higher lumen output than conventional incandescent or CFL lighting systems. Heat pump water heating technologies provide an estimated 7,000 BTU output and a max water temp of 135 while using less than 800 watts nominal. Air Conditioning units using proven ductless-split DC Inverter technologies provide remote controlled zoned cooling while using as little as 1,200 watts for a 11,000BTU system. Energy efficient appliances are readily available and help to reduce overall electrical loads.

Renewable Energy fueled by the new interest in Residential and Commercial Solar PV Systems has a bright future and will dramatically change the landscape of the modern energy grid forever.

The Everything Green Handbook

What is "Going Green" all about?

Uni-Solar PVL installation at Sonoma State University in Rohnert Park, California

Green Streets International
Back in the 1980's a small community in Tacoma, Washington came together and birthed a non-profit organization called Safe Streets. The purpose was to create a grassroots network that encouraged participation, involvement and action to provide safer streets for all members of the community.

Sister Laura Neal, who was actively involved in Safe Streets and was featured in a Public Service Announcement for the organization, is one of the original Founders of Green Streets International.

Green Streets International (GSI) is an organization that provides Free Job Training, Workshops and Job Placement Assistance to our youth who are committed to starting a career in the Green Building Trades, including Alternative Power systems.

GSI is actively seeking to expand it's services to communities in the USA and abroad.

www.GREENSTREETSAMERICA.blogspot.com

Sustainable Development can be achieved by wise and accountable use of natural resources in a manner that meets the needs of the present generation without compromising the ability of future generations to meet their needs in a similar fashion. Certified Green Products allow designers, builders and homeowners the option to identify and select energy saving, environmentally friendly products and services that will help us conserve our valuable natural resources. Sustainable Development requires vision and commitment to follow proven sustainable techniques and adopt the associated proven technologies in an affordable strategy. This Integration has a positive impact on the Global Economy, Environment and Society.

Together with International Public and Private organizations, we're making a concerned effort to reach out to our communities. We look forward to the day when it's commonplace to work in agreement within our local communities, builders, contractors, engineers, designers and prospective homeowners to develop more energy efficient homes, neighborhoods, and venues for this and future generations. The end product will be a shared sense of community ownership, job creation and sustainable communities as we build, what can be referred to as "Pathways to Synergy".

Imagine communities that are 100% energy self-sufficient through the integration of energy efficient designs, solar, wind, geo and hydro power systems. Underground renewable energy power grid connecting each home to a local or remote renewable energy substation. Meandering paths and walkways, scattered amongst tree lined community parks and gathering areas, neighborhood schools that educate and train students in green technology that are adjacent to cluster communities with bike and jogging paths and nearby small shops and retail conveniences within walking distance.

Green Streets International is a Non-Profit group working towards that goal.

The Everything Green Handbook

The Green Advantage

Enhanced Health & Productivity

Clean water, fresh air, low VOC and no off-gassing products should be the benchmark for homes built under the "green" design concept. Energy conservation and eco-friendly homes do not happen by accident, it takes planning and design guidelines to ensure homes provide comfort, style and are also affordable. Choosing off the shelf products that are eco-friendly minimize costs and help decrease the time required to source specialized products that add time and expense to the construction process. Despite the misconception, "green homes" can be stylish, affordable and built on a reduced timeline.

The Protec® Building System is currently used throughout the United States and Hawaii and also in the Caribbean, to build what is described as, "Net Zero Energy Homes". Recently receiving international approval from The Bahamas Ministry of Works, the Protec Building System® is meticulously engineered to design loads of up to 150 mile per winds. According to the information from the website www.BAHAMASSDG.com, these "Net Zero Energy Homes" generate more energy than they consume, have minimal environmental impact, are adaptable to most architectural designs, resist high winds and are very compatible to developers seeking higher construction productivity rates.

Long-Term Economic Returns

Unfortunately, oftentimes when new green initiatives are initially introduced into some regions for the first time, there exists an intense amount of resistance as traditional stakeholders, with entrenched concepts and methods are challenged by the new technologies. However, for the greater good of the communities served, acceptance and embracing advances in proven green technology ensures our nation continued success in the renewable energy and sustainable development sectors.

Reduced Environmental Impact

Waste reduction, resource conservation and maintaining pure water inventories are important issues that face any region, but even more so in coastal areas. As our population grows so does the need to pay more strict attention to the subject of waste management and recycling. Education and acceptance of recycling is the key. Conservation is an adopted lifestyle and our communities must see it as a benefit in order to embrace it. Tangible incentives such as reductions in Waste Collection rates for households that recycle, reduced utility rates for homes with Solar or wind Power Generation systems and reduced municipal water rates for households with Atmospheric Water Generators would go a long way to helping the larger public adopt and embrace "Going Green".

The Everything Green Handbook

BUILDING BLOCKS

The technology exists today, and visionary stakeholders are embracing the concept of green communities and taking a stance to involve themselves in every aspect of the new green economy. The list of organizations, building systems, green products, how-to books and green certifications are endless as more public and private entities see the value in "going green".

The basic building block of developing a green community is the infrastructure and building design; Water, sewage disposal, power, communications and transportation. For every element in the conventional "building block" there is a green alternative. Water needs can be meet by Atmospheric Water Generation and Rain water collection. Onsite sewage demands can be mitigated by the use of approved hybrid composting low-flush toilets. A green underground power grid can feed every home in the cluster community from a remote "energy farm" unique to the geographic area of the community; Solar, Wind, Hydro, Geo or a matrix of each. Neighborhood WiFi services can connect schools, libraries, homes and stores as an integrated service that seamlessly links each cluster community to the major communication vendors at a reduced cost. Transportation becomes an external need, as the cluster community provides access to all community services within the core, accessible by walkways, pathways, and electric vehicle corridors. These communities show that Sustainable Development is more than a "popular catch phrase", it's a "lifestyle".

PATHWAYS TO SYNERGY
BUILDING BLOCKS

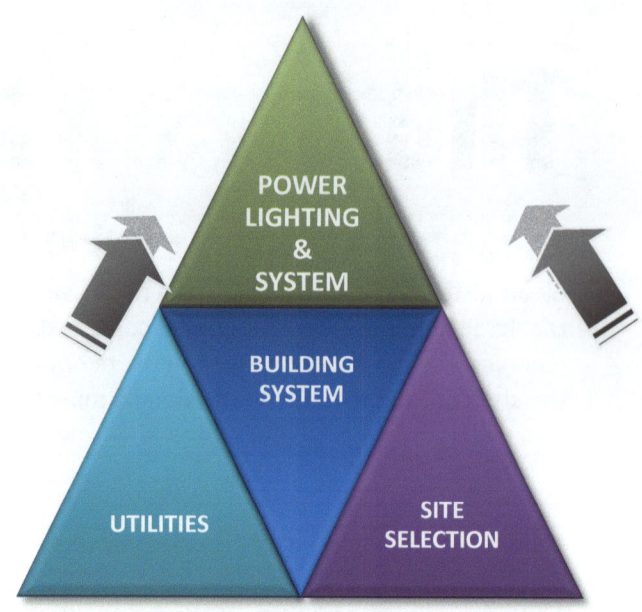

Environment & Community

The basic concept of "Pathways to Synergy" prompts the stakeholders to ask relative questions and formulate a development plan that is in harmony with the 4 Building Blocks and the foundation on which they will be constructed, within the existing environment and local community.

- Within what type of environment are we building?
- Does the local community support Green Technology?
- What utilities are available and at what cost?
- Will the project be 100% Off-Grid or Grid Tied?
- Is the site Zoned and suitable for Green Construction?
- Does the Building Department promote Green Homes?
- Will the Building System meet local building codes?
- Can renewable energy be generated at the site?
- What permits are required for Solar or Wind Systems?

The Everything Green Handbook

SIMPLE RECIPE FOR SUCCESS

- Seek out Public & Private Green Organizations
- Utilize an Approved Building System
- Cooperate with Established Vendors
- Request On-Site Support
- Train and Recruit Local Workforce
- Seek Independent Energy Verification
- Invite Media and Political Organizations
- Promote Community Expositions

Let Green Technology Work For You!

The Unites States Green Building Council, (USGBC) offers an excellent source of Green Community Development information under their Neighborhood Development Resources initiative.

USGBC provides up to date resources for neighborhood planners that want to integrate the principles of smart locations, neighborhood design, and green infrastructure and building design into their development model. Green communities that are designed with the recommendations of established green energy standards have the ability to reduce greenhouse gas emissions from both the building and transportation sectors.

The impact is felt no matter what size your community is. From a small green community of 2 or 3 prospective homeowners that come together and decide they want to create a sustainable community that uses 100% renewable energy to a 400 acres master planned green community complete with electric cars in every garage. These resources provided by the USGBC is a great place to start and introduce yourself to the LEED for Neighborhood Development rating system, as well as a presentation on LEED-ND and case studies on LEED-ND certified projects. Visit them online at www.USGBC.org

Green Economic Recovery Resources

Green building strategies, including energy efficiency, are a cornerstone of the plan to revitalize our economy. Funding provided by the American Recovery and Reinvestment Act of 2009 (ARRA) offers a tremendous opportunity for state and local governments to jump-start green building efforts, create green jobs, and save energy and money. USGBC is committed to helping our communities make the most of this historic opportunity. The following resources and best practices are intended to support state and local leadership and assist governments in these critical efforts.

The American Recovery and Reinvestment Act of 2009, signed into law by President Obama on Feb. 17, 2009, includes a number of provisions that present opportunities for green building and green job creation.

- Recovery.Gov: **www.RECOVERY.gov**
- Department of Education: **www.ED.GOV/recovery**
- Department of Energy: **www.ENERGY.GOV/recovery**
- Department of Housing and Urban Development: **www.HUD.GOV/recovery**
- Department of Labor: **www.DOL.GOV/recovery**

BUILDING SYSTEMS

Building design is an import component of the "Green Building Block". The structure must be energy efficient, structurally sound, acceptable within a wide range of municipalities, affordable as well as being esthetically pleasing.

There are as many building systems and vendors as there are shades of green but for our sample green community project, we have chosen to feature the ProTec® Structural Concrete Insulated Panel manufactured by T.Clear, Corp a USGBC member located in Hamilton, Il.

T. Clear ProTEC® Concrete Structural Insulated Panel System provides a well engineered alternative to conventional lumber framing systems for residential and light commercial structures.

For more information on the ProTEC® Building System visit:

www.TCLEAR.com

Strong, Tight & Easy To Construct

Residential & light commercial buildings constructed with ProTEC® Concrete Structural Insulated Panel Systems are strong and tight. They are energy efficient, resistant to mold and mildew, and environmentally sound. They are, "simply, built to last" as the manufacturer describes in sales literature.

"The walls go up in a fraction of the time it takes for conventional framing. Using simple tools, a small crew can typically erect the walls in a fraction of the time it takes for conventional framing. Because of the Util-A-Crete® facings, time and materials are saved when finishing both the interior and exterior surfaces. ProTEC Panels come standard with pre-cut electrical chases to help speed the wiring operation. This means fewer delays, resulting in a quicker overall construction cycle." ~ T.Clear

Green Housing

We've selected the ProTEC® Building System for the versatility and ease of integration in the development of green communities. Applicable for use in light-commercial and 1 and 2 story residential design, the ProTEC® Building system is our green building system of choice.

- Steel frame with R-20 Insulation and Concrete facings
- Mold and Mildew Resistant
- Moisture and Impact Resistant
- Not prone to Warping, Decay, Swelling or Softening
- Faster Construction Cycles
- Lower Heating & Cooling Costs
- Easy Assembly – Minimum Tool Requirements

The Everything Green Handbook

GREEN HOME PROFILE

PROJECT NAME: Las Casas Verdes
COMMUNITY UNITS: One-Bedroom Cottage
POWER GRID: Solar & Wind with Battery Backup
WATER SYSTEM: AWG and Rain Water Harvesting
REFUSE DISPOSAL: Compost Stations and Recycling
BUILDING SYSTEM: ProTEC® by T.Clear
FLOOR PLAN: www.EPLANS.com

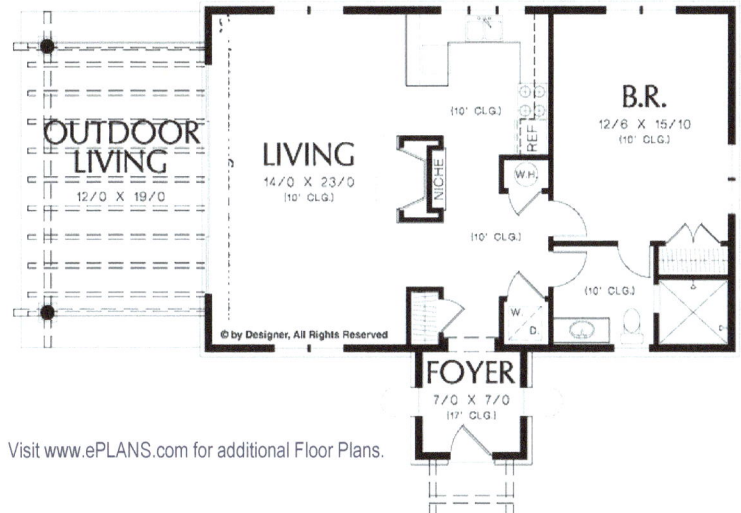

Visit www.ePLANS.com for additional Floor Plans.

PROJECT SCOPE

Construct a 1-Bedroom Cottage with 100% Off-Grid Renewable Energy rain water harvesting, 100 Watt total lighting consumption with minimal Environmental impact at a per/unit Cost of under $80,000 not including Permit Fees.

SOLUTION:

- ProTEC® Structural Concrete Insulated Panels
- BahamaFoam™ Insulated Roofing System
- Pella Low-E Windows
- BahaTech™ Radiant Barrier Exterior Paint
- BahaTech™ LED Lighting System
- Green Floor Plans by Designer, Inc.
- 1.4 kw Solar Patio Cover
- BahaTech ™ Solar-AC 10,000BTU
- (4) x 210 AH AGM Battery Back-up
- Concrete Stamped Concrete Flooring
- Energy Star Appliances
- Whole-House Energy Recovery Ducting
- AWG Water Generator 3 Gal/Day

Lighting Load: 100 Watts - 20 x 5Watt LED
Incidental Load: 2x100W Fans / 1x100w Fan
Cooling Load: 864 Watts – Solar-AC
Appliance Load:

Microwave	1,200W
Dishwasher	1,200W
Refrigerator	650W
Clothes Washer	700W
Heat-Pump Water Heater	680

Misc. Electrical Load: 500W

For information on this project contact:
Email:greendirectusa@gmail.com

Las Casas Verdes CERTIFIED GREEN
SAVES ENERGY | REDUCES WASTE | GLOBAL SOLUTION ™

Through the smart use of LED Lighting, ProTECH® Concrete Insulated Structural Building Panels , Heat-Pump Water Heater, Insulated Foam Roofing and Insulating Ceramic Exterior Paint the Energy usage of each Valencia Home is reduced by as much as 60% when compared to conventional Concrete Block or Wood Frame construction. This energy efficiency savings translates into less demands on the Heating and Cooling system. The 10,000 BTU Solar HVAC unit can easily control the indoor temperature, providing comfort and energy savings.

Energy efficient, minimal environmental impact, structurally sound, affordable and esthetically pleasing, the Valencia is a good example of a project with "Synergy".

The Everything Green Handbook

PATHWAYS TO SYNERGY SOLUTIONS

BASIC ENERGY STANDARDS

Insulation: Surprisingly, this very simple component is often overlooked as the first line of protection to maintain a comfortable indoor climate. R-Values rate the relative thermal properties of Insulation. The higher the R-Value the more resistance to Heat-Flow.

- **Foundation** Perimeter Insulation in colder climates helps to isolate the foundation from below-grade temperatures and translates into lower heating costs.
- **Insulated Exterior Walls** will increase the comfort level of the indoor temperature and will help to lower your Heating and Cooling expenses.
- **Attic Insulation** is a must for proper insulation and thermal protection of your residence. Loose Fill, Batts or Spray Foam should be used to keep your Heating and Cooling costs at their lowest possible levels.

Radiant Barrier: Radiant barriers are typically installed in attic areas to reduce intense summer heat gain in hot arid environments and winter heat loss in colder climates, which helps lower your heating and cooling expenses. The barriers consist of a highly reflective material that reflects radiant heat rather than absorbing it. Typically sold as a reflective foil, reflective metal roof shingles or reflective laminated roof sheathing in 4' x 8' x ½" or 4' x 8' x 5/8" dimensions.

Caulking & Sealing: Air leakage occurs when a home does not have adequate caulking and weather-stripping to alleviate drafts from penetrations in the exterior walls. A sure way to save "Energy Dollars" is to investing proper sealing of your home. Here are some of the most commonly overlooked areas of Air Leakage :

- Caulk and Weather-Strip Window & Door Frames
- Check the area around Dryer Vents
- Electrical, Telephone and Cable penetrations
- Around Hose Bibs, Water and Gas Lines

Money invested in sealing your home from energy wasting drafts will pay big dividends as lower "energy costs".

WHAT'S THE CO$T

Installing R-49 Attic Insulation costs an average of $0.94/sq ft including Material & Labor nationally. Contractor rates in your specific area may vary.

Check average rates in your area by visiting:

http://www.ORNL.GOV/~roofs/Zip/

This handy online resource provided by the Department of Energy lists recommendations for insulation based on your Zip Code and provides average costs per square foot.

GREEN COMMUNITIES DEVELOPMENT

Solar Power Systems
Solar Air Conditioning
Portable Solar Power Units
Water from AIR AWG Systems
Sustainable Development
Community Training Programs
Consulting and Project Mgt.

Palm Springs, CA

The Everything Green Handbook

4-WATT LED BULB

Has Equivalent Illumination & Consumes Less Energy Compared to

13 Watt CFL

40 Watt Incandescent

PATHWAYS TO SYNERGY

MINIMUM ENERGY STANDARDS

Energy Efficient Low-E Windows: Another area to pay close attention is the energy efficiency of your windows. Referred to as Low-E (Emissivity), windows that have an applied metal or metallic oxide coating reduce radiated heat flow through the glass and into your home. The various coatings are virtually transparent to visible light. Installing Double-pane Low-E Windows are a great start towards energy efficiency for your home.

- **U-Value:** A simple way to rate energy efficiency of window is by U-Value. Keep in mind that lower U-Values have better insulating values. A value of +/- 0.40 is typical for an area of moderate Air Conditioning requirements.
- **Solar Heat Gain Coefficient (SHGC):** When comparing windows by SHGC, you're evaluating a window on how well it blocks the radiated heat of the sun. In warm climates a low SHGC is a benefit. However, in the harsh cold of Northern Climates, consideration should be given to allowing for a slightly higher SHGC of +/- .55 to allow natural solar heat gain in the Winter.

Energy Star Appliances: "Qualified Energy Star appliances incorporate advanced technologies that use 10–50% less energy and water than standard models." Visit **www.ENERGYSTAR.gov** for a list of Qualified Products and Manufacturers.

LED Lighting: Here's a very simple Do-it-Yourself project to "GO GREEN" and save your hard earned energy dollars. Convert your Incandescent and CFL Bulbs to LED Lighting. It's been shown that LED lighting uses at least 75% less energy, lasts longer than incandescent and CFL lighting and is available in Cool White, Warm White, and White color range.

LED Lighting is available in many common configurations including 1', 2', 4' & 8' T-8 and T-5 Tubes, Globes, Candelabra, Recessed, MR16 and GU-10, Standard Base E-26 and E-27 Bulbs.

For more information on Residential and Commercial LED Lighting Solutions visit www.OFFGRIDLED.COM

The Everything Green Handbook

"GREEN HOME" | Systems Integration

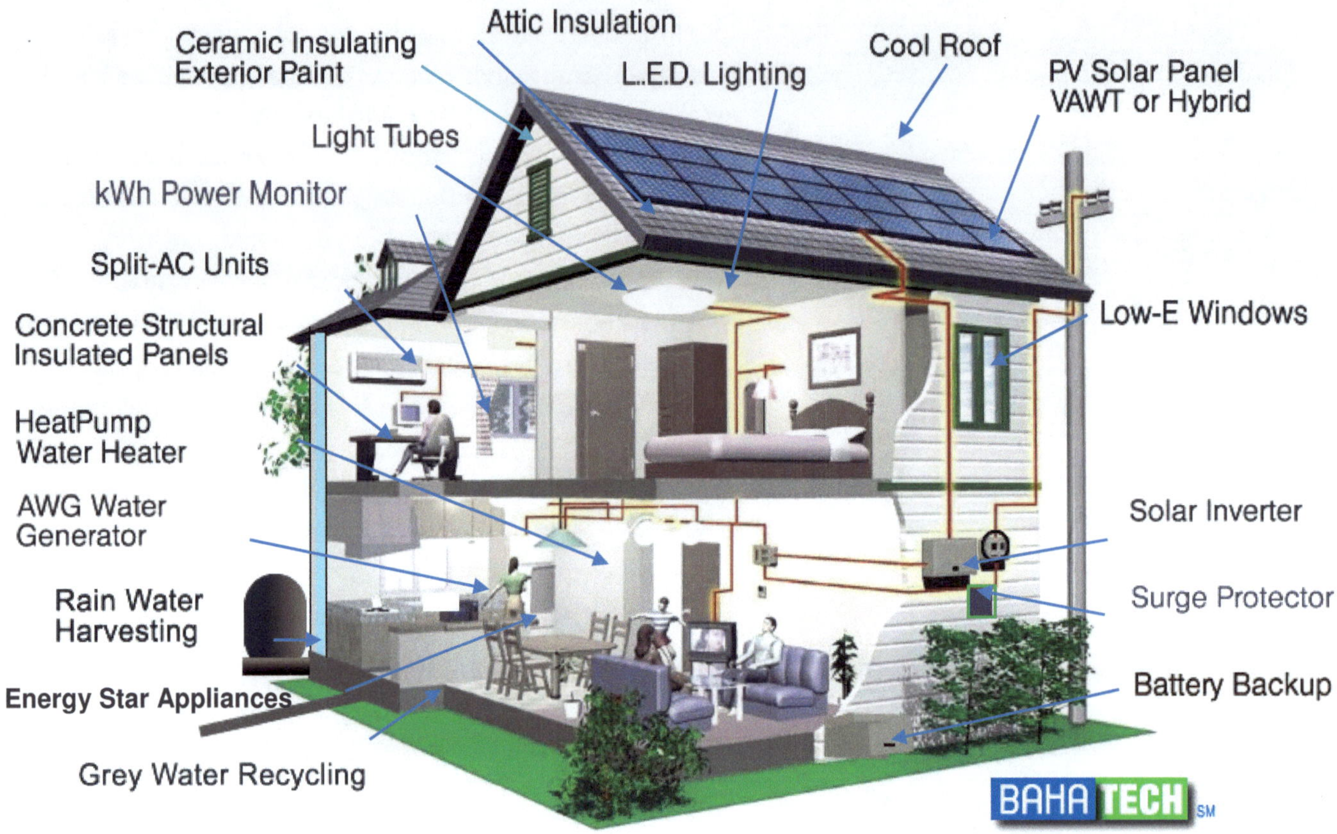

Diagram labels:
- Ceramic Insulating Exterior Paint
- Attic Insulation
- L.E.D. Lighting
- Cool Roof
- PV Solar Panel VAWT or Hybrid
- Light Tubes
- kWh Power Monitor
- Split-AC Units
- Concrete Structural Insulated Panels
- HeatPump Water Heater
- AWG Water Generator
- Rain Water Harvesting
- Energy Star Appliances
- Grey Water Recycling
- Low-E Windows
- Solar Inverter
- Surge Protector
- Battery Backup

CERTIFIED GREEN — SAVES ENERGY | REDUCES WASTE | GLOBAL SOLUTION ™

Sustainable Home Design | GCD | Green Communities Development

BAHA TECH℠

GREEN SURFING

One of the most simple "Pathways to Synergy" is the integration of off-the-shelf conservation and energy saving products that are just a click away from most homeowners. There is a wealth of information available online for fast and simple fact finding, opening the doorways to hundreds of affordable "Green" products and systems you can easily add to your existing home or integrate into plans for building your own "Green Home"!

www.ENERGYSTAR.gov

The Everything Green Handbook

PATHWAYS TO SYNERGY SOLUTIONS

POWER

WATER FACT:
Did you know that 1 inch of rainfall on a 2,000 sq. ft. roof generates an estimated 1,200 gallons of water?

Rain Water Harvesting is not only simple and practical, but it's also affordable.

UTILITIES

SITE SELECTION

1.8KW SOLAR POWER SYSTEM ~ 1,000 WATT COMPACT WIND TURBINE

Designed for high reliability, adaptability to a wide variations of climate zones and ease of installation this 1.8kW Solar Power system uses 185Watt Rigid Frame Solar Panels, Pure-Sine Wave Inverter with reserve power supplied by 210 AH - AGM 12VDC Batteries.

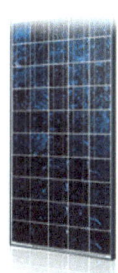

185 Watt Solar PV Panel | 1,000 Watt Wind Turbine | 210 AH AGM 12VDC Batteries

SYSTEM DESIGN & SUPPLIER
BahaTec™ www.BAHAMASSDG.com

Water & Sewage Disposal, Site Features & Orientation

Municipal water was available at the selected site which was chosen for it's natural vegetation, moderate elevation for wind power generation and southern solar exposure. Residential water usage is minimized by the use of 3-Stage Filtered Rain Water Harvesting for washing Clothes, Showering and for Kitchen and Toilet water supply. Additionally, an Atmospheric Water Generator was selected for the production of up to 5-Gals/Day of drinking water. Hybrid-Toilets with composting features and a grey water recycling systems are both used to dramatically reduce on-site sewage outflows to a traditional septic tank system.

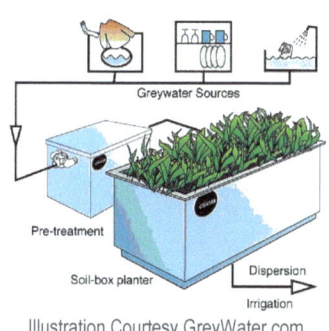

Illustration Courtesy GreyWater.com | Gator Pro® Grey Water Diversion System | BioLet® Composting Toilet

www.GREYWATER.com | www.gatorpro.com.au/ | www.BIOLET.com

15

PATHWAYS TO SYNERGY SOLUTIONS

100 Watts Total Lighting Load

The advantages of switching to LED light bulbs are that LED Bulbs have a much smaller environmental footprint. Less energy used, and less trash in our landfills due to a longer life and fewer replacements are both very compelling reasons for eco-conscious buyers to make the shift. We have managed to provide lighting for the entire Green Model Cottage, interior and exterior with only 100Watts of LED Lighting. Remote controlled and dimmable, these bulbs reduce lighting loads by as much as 70% when compared to CFL Bulbs.

LED LIGHTING

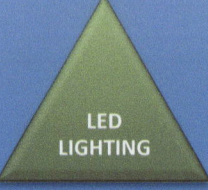   

4 CREE® Bulbs	8 CREE® Bulbs	8 CREE® Bulbs
5Watt Par x **4**= 20W	5-Watt x **8**= 40 W	5-Watt Recessed x **8**= 40W

SUPPLIER
Innovations LED Lighting
International Dealer www.BAHAMASSDG.com

Structural Concrete Insulated Building Panels

T. Clear ProTEC® Concrete Structural Insulated Panel System provides a well engineered alternative to conventional lumber framing systems for residential and light commercial structures.

BUILDING SYSTEM

   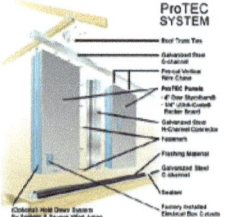 

The walls go up in a fraction of the time it takes for conventional framing.
Using simple tools, a small crew can typically erect the walls in a fraction of the time it takes for conventional framing. Because of the Util-A-Crete® facings, time and materials are saved when finishing both the interior and exterior surfaces. ProTEC Panels come standard with pre-cut electrical chases to help speed the wiring operation. This means fewer delays, resulting in a quicker overall construction cycle.

SUPPLIER
Authorized ProTec® Dealer
Green Communities Development Tel: 206-339-0797

The Everything Green Handbook

Solar Power is on the Move!

Table 3.2 Annual Photovoltaic Domestic Shipments, 1998 - 2007

Year	Photovoltaic Cells and Modules[1]
1998	15,069
1999	21,201
2000	19,838
2001	36,310
2002	45,313
2003	48,664
2004	78,346
2005	134,465
2006	206,511
2007	280,475
U.S. Total	886,193

[1]Total shipments minus export shipments.
Notes: Totals may not equal sum of components due to independent rounding.
Total shipments include those made in or shipped to U.S. Territories.
Source: Energy Information Administration, Form EIA-63B, "Annual Photovoltaic Module/Cell Manufacturers Survey."

Source: National Renewable Energy Laboratory, Photographic Information Exchange.

In 2010, the use of Renewable Energy is being supported, encouraged and promoted in the United States like never before. There aren't many of us who haven't heard the term "going green" and know it's meaning. Just as the use of renewable energy is gaining ground in the United States, DSIRE a comprehensive online Database of State Incentives for Renewables and Efficiencies was launched. This handy source of information on state, local, utility, and federal incentives and policies promotes renewable energy and energy efficiencies in the U.S. Established in 1995 and funded by the U.S. Department of Energy, DSIRE is an ongoing project of the N.C. Solar Center and the Interstate Renewable Energy Council.

SOURCE: 2009 N.C. Solar Center / N.C. State University / College of Engineering

Featured above is header page from the DSIRE Website detailing the incentives currently available for the State of New York. To check the Federal and State incentives available in your area visit: www.**DSIREUSA**.org

The Everything Green Handbook

SOLAR ENERGY SHOWCASE

Photos Courtesy of National Renewable Energy Laboratory — www.NREL.gov

Designed for grid-connected applications, these solar modules from BP Solar grace the entrance of this 2007 Solar Decathlon competition home. With a rated power of 190W, bypass diodes limit the loss of energy in the event of partial shadowing.

"Courtesy of DOE/NREL, Credit – Jim Tetro."

21st Century Performance home built by Centex with the Davis Energy Group as part of DOE's Zero Energy Homes initiative combines state-of-the-art energy efficient construction with solar hot water and solar electric systems to significantly reduce the amount of energy required from the local utility. The house is in Centex's Los Olivos community in Livermore, California.

"Courtesy of DOE/NREL, Credit – David Springer."

The Everything Green Handbook

SOLAR ENERGY SHOWCASE

Photos Courtesy of National Renewable Energy Laboratory —www.NREL.gov

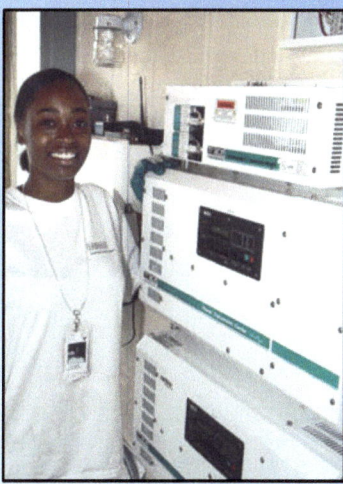

SOLAR DECATHALON: Looking East Toward The Capitol, a quiet moment in the Solar Village, with the Capitol in the background. Hundreds of curious spectators will pass through in the afternoon hours. Tuskegee University's house can be seen in the foreground on the left. On the right, a Tuskegee University student works on the team's power conditioning equipment to maximize efficiency.

"Courtesy of DOE/NREL, Credit – Warren Gretz"

National Technology Day and Media Event: Local elementary school students check out one of the interactive displays in the Solar Village.

"Courtesy of DOE/NREL, Credit – Warren Gretz"

The Everything Green Handbook

WIND ENERGY SHOWCASE

Photos Courtesy of National Renewable Energy Laboratory   www.NREL.gov

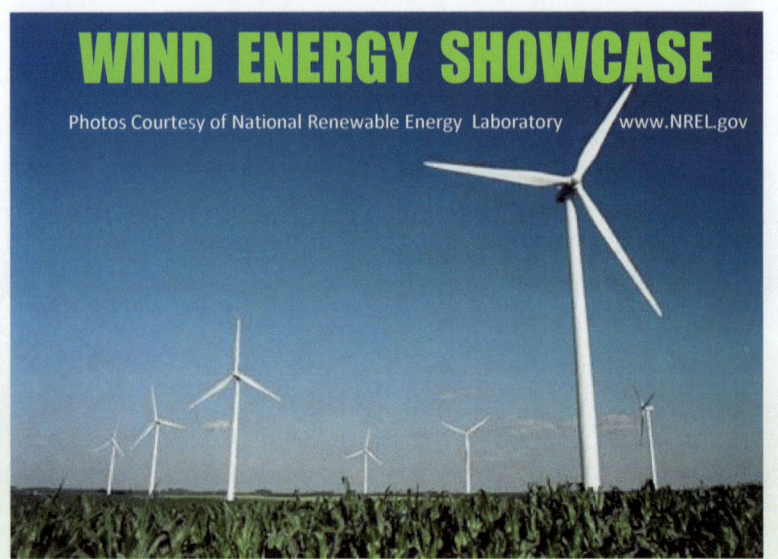

The G. McNeilus Wind Farm is located just south of the City of Adams, Minnesota. Garwin Mcneilus, an industrial tycoon, know for his manufacturing of ready mix trucks, is a strong supporter of renewable energy. Initially, 9 NEG Micon 1.5 turbines were erected, producing 13.5 MW in 2003, which has since been expanded. The power is sold to Dairyland Cooperative, with the profits of one of the turbines being donated by the McNeilus family to an orphanage in India for blind children. The land loss incurred by the local farmers to the wind turbines in only 4 Acres
"Courtesy of Todd Spink"

Maple Ridge Wind Farm
Lewis County, New York.
"Courtesy Iberdrola Renewables, Inc. (formerly PPM Energy, Inc.)"

On September 10, 2007, the City of Berkeley installed its first small-scale wind turbine t power the city's Shorebird Park Nature Center at the Berkeley marina. The Turbine powers the Center's Green Classroom. The turbine, the Skystream 3.7 from Southwest Windpower, is a new backyard-scale wind turbine designed for rid-connected residential homes. Depending on the wind, Skystream generates between 30-80% of the power used by a typical home. Typically, Skystream is installed on lots sized 1/2 to two acres, or on properties with adequate wind.

The City of Berkeley's Shorebird Park Nature Center is the first city-owned straw bale building in the United States. It has a solar hot water system to provide heating year-round in the cool marina climate, and a solar electric system to power the aquariums computers, lighting and other equipment.   *"Photo Courtesy of Southwest Windpower"*

The Everything Green Handbook

WIND POWER

20% by 2030

Wind power could provide 20% of U.S. electricity needs by 2030, according to a DOE report titled "20% Wind Energy by 2030: Increasing Wind Energy's Contribution to U.S. Electricity Supply." The report identifies the steps that need to be addressed to reach the 20% goal, including reducing the cost of wind technologies, building new transmission infrastructure, and enhancing domestic manufacturing capability.

Wind Powering America is a commitment to dramatically increase the use of wind energy in the United States. This initiative will establish new sources of income for American farmers, Native Americans, and other rural landowners, and meet the growing demand for clean sources of electricity.

Through Wind Powering America, the United States will achieve targeted regional economic development, enhance our power generation options, protect the local environment, and increase our energy and national security. Visit www.**windpoweringamerica**.gov for detailed information on Wind Power programs in the U.S.A.

SOURCE: U.S. Department of Energy – www.windpoweringamerica.gov

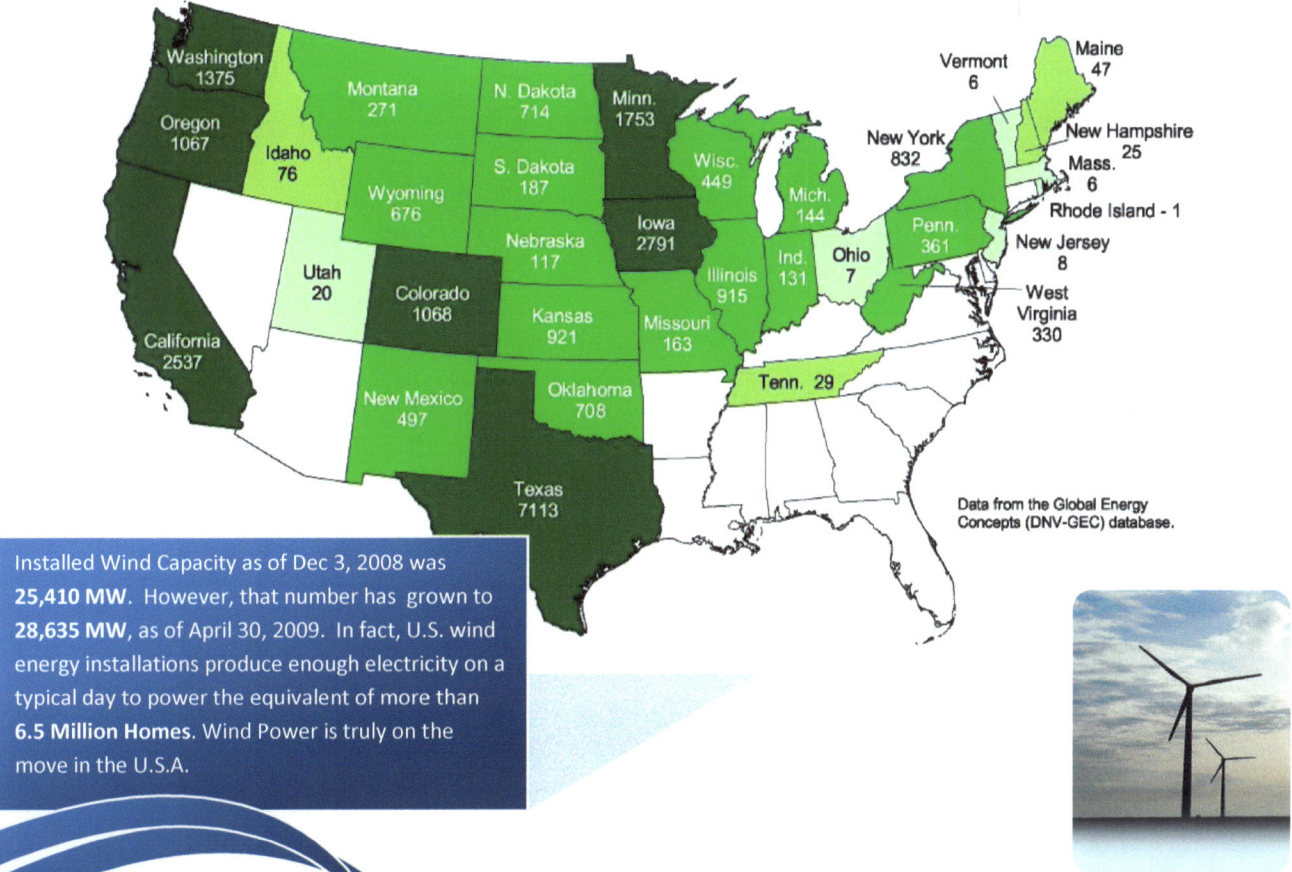

Data from the Global Energy Concepts (DNV-GEC) database.

Installed Wind Capacity as of Dec 3, 2008 was **25,410 MW**. However, that number has grown to **28,635 MW**, as of April 30, 2009. In fact, U.S. wind energy installations produce enough electricity on a typical day to power the equivalent of more than **6.5 Million Homes**. Wind Power is truly on the move in the U.S.A.

The Everything Green Handbook

EV SHOWCASE

Photos Courtesy of National Renewable Energy Laboratory www.NREL.gov

NREL's Plug-in Hybrid Electric Vehicle (PHEV), with wind turbine, at the National Wind Technology Center (NWTC).

"Courtesy Mike Linenberger Golden, Colorado- National Renewable Energy Laboratory- National Wind Technology Center- NWTC"

SUMMIT OF THE EIGHT ADVANCED VEHICLES SHOWCASE. Recharging a Toyota RAV4 Electric Vehicle (EV) - Denver, Colorado- Denver Convention Center

"Courtesy Warren Gretz"

IndyGo hybrid Electric Transit Bus Manufactured by Ebus, Inc.

"Courtesy Leslie Eudy - Freedom Car and Vehicle Technologies Program, Advanced Vehicle Testing Activity."

ΩMEGA ELECTRIC MOTORCARS™

Test Driving an Omega Electric MotorCars' 2-Door VMX EV.

"Courtesy Omega Electric Motorcars"

The Everything Green Handbook

22

PATHWAYS TO SYNERGY
jobs | training | prosperity

U.S. DEPARTMENT OF ENERGY
Energy Efficiency & Renewable Energy
www.EERE.ENERGY.gov
A prime resource for a wide range of topics including Biomass, Geothermal, Hydrogen & Fuel Cells, Solar, Electric Vehicles, Weatherization, Wind and Hydropower.

"Courtesy Department of Energy"
Visit: http://www1.eere.energy.gov/education/other_jobs.html

THE BUSINESS OF SOLAR
Have you owned or operated a Small Business in the past? Interested in becoming a Solar Power System Dealer in the USA or abroad?
Call: 206-339-3797 to Register by Phone
www.GREENCAREERCHANGE.blogspot.com

GREEN HOUSING VOLUNTEERS

www.HABITAT.ORG/getinv/
Join in the fight against poverty housing and homelessness around the world!

GREEN EMPLOYMENT RESOURCES

www.CAREERSINWIND.com
Provides links to employers in the wind energy industry.

www.GREENENERGYJOBS.com
Follow this link for a listing of jobs in the renewable energy industry.

www.GREENJOBS.com
This site lists a wide range of jobs in the clean energy sector in the U.S. and internationally. Positions run the gamut from engineering specialists to program managers and interns.

The Everything Green Handbook

ProTec® by  in CALIFORNIA

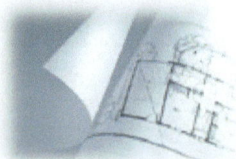

Envision a small housing community that generates it's own electrical power. Homes are designed and integrated to blend with the environment with minimal impact and are esthetically pleasing . Home ownership is made more affordable through the use of an energy efficient building system which also reduces construction waste, lowers labor costs and are simple to erect.

The sequence of photos to the left depicts the construction of a 1,500 Sq. ft. Home in Southern California using Protec® Structural Concrete Insulated Panels manufactured by T. Clear Corp. , Hamilton, Ohio. The crew of four erected all of the exterior and garage walls in less than 3-days.

"Using the ProTec® System we discovered it's a simple installation, with less labor, it's structurally sound and cost effective to build. It's our first and only choice when considering building "Green Homes" for our clients.

The ProTec® Panels compliment the energy package we include in each home we build. The Solar Power System and integrated Solar Patio Covers by 4th Generation Solar, based in Baldwin Park, California supply clean, quiet, renewable energy and when coupled with the LED Lighting System by Innovations LED Lighting, Nassau, Bahamas, we have one of the most energy efficient Home offerings in Southern California." Green Communities Development

Green Communities Development has recently organized a Green Home Training program for Contractors and Residential Framers in Southern California. Protec® panels are also being used to construct Energy Efficient homes in The Bahamas by, So-LarABL Holdings Limited, an innovative development group based in Nassau, Bahamas.

Photos Courtesy Green Communities Development

The Everything Green Handbook

Green Career Change Initiative

There are new and exciting opportunities opening across the USA for talented, creative, business-minded, men and women that want to start their own business. Formulate your plan, Get Trained, Get Empowered and Prosper! Many new start-ups are on the leading edge of "green" technology such as Solar Power, Compact Wind Turbines, LED Lighting, Fuel Cell Technology, Green Home Kits , (LSEV) Electric Vehicles and many other innovative Residential and Commercial Energy Saving products.

The "Green Career Change" Initiative is all about empowering young men and women to begin a New Career as a leader in Managing Businesses, Sales, Marketing , Installation and Service of Green Products and Technologies.

One public agency tasked with the mission to help small emerging businesses receive the tools needed to succeed is the Small Business Administration. The SBA helps Americans start, build and grow businesses. Through an extensive network of field offices and partnerships with public and private organizations, SBA delivers its services to people throughout the United States, Puerto Rico, the U. S. Virgin Islands and Guam.

The U.S. Small Business Administration (SBA) was created in 1953 as an independent agency of the federal government to aid, counsel, assist and protect the interests of small business concerns, to preserve free competitive enterprise and to maintain and strengthen the overall economy of our nation. For example , the SBA offers Guaranteed Loan Programs, some of which are listed below.

7(a) Loan Program:
This is SBA's primary and most flexible loan program, with financing guaranteed for a variety of general business purposes. It is designed for start-up and existing small businesses, and is delivered through commercial lending institutions.

CDC/504 Loan Program:
This program provides long-term, fixed-rate financing to acquire fixed assets (such as real estate or equipment) for expansion or modernization. It is designed for small businesses requiring "brick and mortar" financing, and is delivered by CDCs (Certified Development Companies)—private, non-profit corporations set up to contribute to the economic development of their communities.

Microloan Program:
The Microloan program provides small (up to $35,000) short-term loans for working capital or the purchase of inventory, supplies, furniture, fixtures, machinery and/or equipment. It is designed for small businesses and not-for-profit child-care centers needing small-scale financing and technical assistance for start-up or expansion, and is delivered through specially designated intermediary lenders (nonprofit organizations with experience in lending and technical assistance).

For more information about the services offered by the SBA Visit online at:
www.SBA.gov

Green Scenes

From Top Left to Right:
Solar Street Lamp, Solar Powered Barn, Solar Farm, 100% Electric Vehicle, ProTec® Building System, Palm Springs, CA - Wind Farm

GREEN Lighting Ideas

LED Lighting represents an excellent opportunity for commercial and residential users to achieve additional energy savings when compared to traditional lighting options. Refer to the chart below for a general estimate of Rated Bulb Life.

LIGHT SOURCE	ESTIMATED RANGE OF RATED LIFE
Incandescent	750-2,000
Halogen Incandescent	3,000-4,000
Compact Fluorescent (CFL)	8,000-10,000
Metal Halide	7,500-20,000
Linear Fluorescent	20,000 – 30,000
High-Power White LED	**35,000 – 50,000**

For more information visit www.OFFGRIDLED.com

PRODUCT PROFILES

LED FLOURESCENT
REPLACEMENT BULB

NO BALLASTS REQUIRED

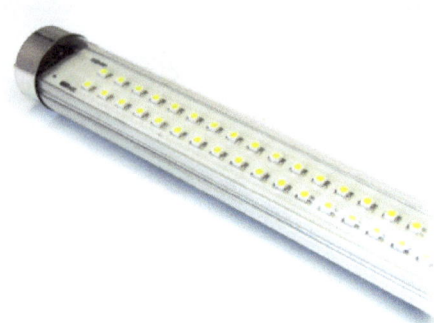

Off Grid LED
www.OffGridLED.com

Features:
Power Consumption: 22W
LED Model: OGL22
LED Quantity: 360pcs
LED Fluorescent Light output: 2200-2350LM
Color Temperature: Warm White:2200-3500K
Pure White:4500-4500K
Cool White:6000-6500K
·Lens type: Transparent Lens, Frosted Lens, Ribbed Lens
·Length: T8-1200mm   Replacement for Standard 48" Tube
·Input Voltage: 85-300V AC or 12V or 24V DC
·Aluminum Alloy Heat Sink
·CE & ROHS approvals

Energy Saving 60% + Compared to Fluorescent Tube
Solid Lighting Source
No UV
No Infrared Light
No Mercury
Lumen Reduction 30% after 30,000h
Working temperature: -40℃～50℃
Constant current led driver
50000h   Long Life Bulb
Lengths: 12" , 24" and 48"

Applications:
·Hospital
·Display Lighting
·Commercial Complexes
·Factories/Offices
·Super-Markets
·Residential/Institution buildings

PRODUCT PROFILES

Charge Controller

MORNINGSTAR SUNKEEPER SK-12
Relay Type Charge Controller

Morningstar's SunKeeper SK-12 solar controller provides a low cost regulated output directly from the solar module to maximize battery life in small solar power applications. The SunKeeper is epoxy encapsulated and rated for outdoor use. By mounting directly to the module junction box and wiring through the junction box knockout, the connection is weather-proof. This eliminates the need for an additional housing for the controller. To withstand the high temperatures at the solar module, the controller has been designed using extremely efficient power electronics and is rated to 70°C. The SunKeeper is also certified for use in Class 1, Division 2 hazardous locations, making it an ideal controller for solar powered oil/gas applications.

FEATURES

- **High Reliability** - Rated to 70°C to operate in high temperatures at the solar module. More reliable than controllers mounted inside the junction box. Uses very low on-resistance power MOSFET's. No need to re-rate.

- **Outdoor Rated** - ETL approved for outdoor use without an additional enclosure.

- **Rugged** - IP65, UV resistant case. Epoxy encapsulated printed circuit board and watertight connection to the module junction box.

- **Extensive Electronic Protections** - Fully protected against reverse polarity, short circuit, over current, lightning and transient surges, high temperature and reverse current at night.

- **Longer Battery Life** - Series PWM with 3 stage charging: bulk, PWM regulation and float. Includes temperature compensation at the controller or alternatively at the battery when using optional remote temperature sensor. Able to charge a zero voltage battery.

- **Rated for Hazardous Locations** - Specifically designed for solar power systems in the oil/gas industry. Approved for use in Class 1, Division 2, Groups A,B,C,D.

- **More Information** - Bi-color LED is easy to read from the ground when the solar module is pole-mounted. Indicates solar charging, regulation, normal nighttime operation and any controller or system faults.

- **Easy to Install** - Fits standard half inch conduit knockout (PG 13.5, M20) in module junction box. Quickly fastens with included locknut. Wires have fork connectors for easy connection to solar module terminals

Mechanical
Power Wires (red-yellow-black) 2.0 mm2 / 14 AWG
RTS Wire Loop (blue) 0.13 mm2 / 22 AWG
Leads Conductor Material Copper
Weight 0.11 kg / 0.25 lbs
Dimensions 99x51x13 mm / 3.9x2.0x0.5 in
Knockout Size M20 / PG 13.5 / ½ "

Environmental
Ambient Temperature Range
-40 C / -40 F to 70C / 158 F
Storage Temperature Range
-55C / -67 F to 85C / 185 F
Humidity 100 %

Electrical Specifications
Nominal System Voltage 12 V
Maximum Solar Input Voltage 30 V
Rated Solar Input:
SK-6   6A
SK-12 12A
Self-consumption Current < 7.0 mA (charging)
~2.0 mA (night)
Battery Operating Range 0 – 15 V
Battery Charging Set Points
Regulation Voltage 14.10 V (@ 25C)
Float Voltage 13.70 V (@ 25C)
Temperature Compensation -30 mV / C
Maximum Charge Voltage Limit 15V

PRODUCT PROFILES

Thin Film Solar

UNSI-SOLAR® THIN FILM SOLAR PANELS
- High Temperature and Low Light Performance
- 20 Year Warranty on Power Output at 80 %
- Multi-Contact Connectors or Junction Box
- Bypass Diodes for Shadow Tolerance
- UL Listed to 600 VDC
- Meets IEC 61646 Requirements

Qualifications and Safety
Listed by Underwriter's Laboratories for electrical and fire safety (Class A Max. Slope 2/12, Class B Max. Slope 3/12, Class C Unlimited Slope fire ratings) for use in systems up to 600 VDC.

:

Application Criterion
- New or qualified new roof installations
- 400 mm (16") minimum steel pan width
- PVDF Coated (Galvalume® or Zincalume® steel metal pan)
- Steel pans with flat surface
- Install by certified installers
- Installation temperature between 10 °C - 40 °C (50 °F - 100 °F)
- Maximum roof temperature 85 °C (185 °F)
- Minimum slope 1:12 (5°)
- Maximum slope 21:12 (60°)

Electrical Specifications STC
(Standard Test Conditions)
(1000 W/m2, AM 1.5, 25 °C Cell Temperature)
Maximum Power (Pmax): 136 W
Voltage at Pmax (Vmp): 33.0 V
Current at Pmax (Imp): 4.1 A
Short-circuit Current (Isc): 5.1 A
Open-circuit Voltage (Voc): 46.2 V
Maximum Series Fuse Rating: 8 A

Performance Characteristics
Rated Power (Pmax): 136 Wp
Production Tolerance: ± 5 %

Environmental
Ambient Temperature Range
-40 C / -40 F to 70C / 158 F
Storage Temperature Range
-55C / -67 F to 85C / 185 F
Humidity 100 %

Construction Characteristics
Dimensions: Length: 5486 mm (216")
Width: 394 mm (15.5")
Depth: 4 mm (0.2") 16 mm (0.6")
Weight: 7.7 kg (17.0 lbs)
Output Cables: ~2.5 mm2 (MC®) Cable
Weatherproof DC Rated
By-pass Diodes:
Connected across every solar cell
Laminate Encapsulation:
Durable ETFE (e.g. Tefzel®)
Adhesive: Ethylene propylene copolymer adhesive-sealant with microbial inhibitor
Cell Type: 22 triple junction amorphous Silicon Solar Cells 356 x 239 mm
(14" x 9.4") Connected in Series

Notes:
1. During the first 8-10 weeks of operation, electrical output exceeds specified ratings. Power output may be higher by 15 %, operating voltage may be higher by 11 % and operating current may be higher by 4 %.
2. Electrical specifications (± 5 %) are based on measurements performed at standard test conditions of 1000 W/m2 irradiance, Air Mass 1.5, and cell temperature of 25 °C after stabilization.
3. Actual performance may vary up to 10 % from rated power due to low temperature operation, spectral and other related effects. Maximum system open-circuit voltage not to exceed 600 VDC per UL.

PRODUCT PROFILES

LED SECURITY LIGHT &
Solar Power System

Item	Solar Powered LED Security Lighting
Lamp Type	LED – Innovations LED Lighting
Federal Tax Rebate	Yes* Subject to Verification
Photocell	Included
Socket Type	Mogul E40
Voltage	120
Lamp Watts	30 Watt CREE ®
Reflector Material	Aluminum
Housing Material	Die Cast Aluminum
Mounting	Wall
Housing Finish	Bronze
Includes	Lamp, Mounting Hardware, Photocell
Lamp Included	Yes
Description/Special Features	Industrial Grade
Ambient Temp. Range (F)	-22 to 120
Light Distribution	Type V
Length (In.)	15-1/2
Width (In.)	13
Height (In.)	17
Standards	UL Listed for Wet Locations
Runtime	13 Hours – Dusk/Dawn

FEATURES

Solar Powered
Battery Backup System - Dusk/Dawn
Integrated Photocell
Bronze Housing
Wall Mount or Pole Mounted
Waterproof Housing
Shatter Resistant Lens
LED Solid State Bulb
No Mercury
No Ballast or Starter
LED EZ-Install System ™
Lightweight
2-Year Bulb Replacement Guarantee

Available in Cobra Head Format

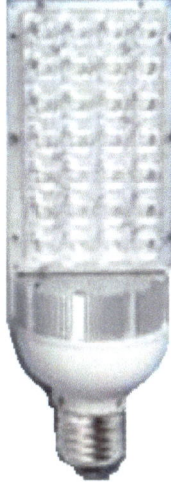

www.OffGridLED.com

PRODUCT PROFILES

AGM Battery Technology

According to Wikipedia, "AGM Batteries were developed by Concorde Aircraft Battery, in the late 1980s in San Bernardino California. The AGM battery technology was pioneered to be a warm weather, vibration resistant, and chemical alternative to the expensive Ni-Cad batteries in both Naval Helicopters and Fighter Aircraft. As production was mechanized, Optima Battery patented a spiral wound method for producing an AGM battery. Due to the spiral wound cell configuration, they are also sometimes referred to as spiral wound. These two manufacturers maintain both UL, CE, and Mil-Spec ratings on their genuine AGM Batteries."

ADVANTAGES

All AGM batteries boast significant performance enhancement over traditional flooded lead acid cells:

- AGM Batteries are un-spillable, keeping lead and acid out of the environment.

- AGM Batteries have very low internal resistance allowing them to be charged and discharged quite rapidly without creating heat based on construction and pure lead.

- AGM Batteries are maintenance free, never requiring a watering over the life of the battery.

- AGM Batteries will not corrode their surroundings as the acid is encapsulated in the matting.

- AGM Batteries will not freeze and crack, operating well below 0°F or C.

- AGM Batteries can be UL, DOT, CE, Coast Guard, and Mil-Spec approved to isolate HAZ-MAT.

PRODUCT PROFILES

PORTABLE SOLAR POWER
EMERGENCY POWER

DPK+™
SOLAR POWERED DISASTER PREPAREDNES POWER KIT

During unforeseen circumstances when the Power Goes Off, whether due to a National Disaster or unscheduled Power Outage, homeowners can have a level of Safety and Security the DPK+™ provides which includes these standard features below.

Large capacity generators are also available up to a rated Inverter Capacity of 4,500 Watts. Thin-Film and Framed PV Panels are included . Assembled in the USA and Bahamas.

- Portable 600 Watt Power System
- Built-in Lamp & Simple Pushbutton Operation
- AM/FM Radio +Digital Alarm Clock
- Provides Extended lighting for Emergency use
- 40 Watt Solar Panel for Renewable Charging
- Accessories including Cables, 12VDC & 110VAC Charger
- 110VAC Power Outlets
- 25' Grounded Extension Chord
- Powers AC & DC Appliances

AC/DC-Powered Products Watts Average Runtime for the 600 Watt DPK+*

- Cordless Telephone — 5 Watts 56 Hours
- Fluorescent Work Light — 14Watts 20 Hours
- Laptop Computer — 80Watts 3.5 Hours
- "LED" Table Lamp — 40Watt Equivalent 60 Hours
- 13" Color TV — 60Watts 4.5 Hours
- 3/8" Drill — 190 Watts 50 min.
- DC Oscillating Fan — 60 Watts 4.5 Hours

For more information on this and other Energy Saving Products powered by Clean Solar Power Off Grid LED at 206-339-3797. The DPK+ Logo and Trademark are the property of Green Direct USA

PRODUCT PROFILES

Water from AIR?

A Unique Water Generation System

The concept is simple and has been used for decades. An **Atmospheric Water Generator (AWG)**, is a device that extracts water from humid ambient air. Water vapor in the air is condensed by cooling the air below its dew point under pressure and collecting and further filtering the water for potable uses. Unlike a dehumidifier, an AWG is designed to render the water potable. AWGs are very useful in locations where pure drinking water is difficult or impossible to obtain, as there is almost always a small amount of water in the air that can be harvested and collected as a drinking water resource.

Green Direct USA ™ has taken AWG technology one step further by adding a Small Solar Power Generator to the System which allows the unit to run 100% from Clean Solar Power. An additional benefit is the Electrical Power Generation. So remote locations can now benefit from a clean source of Water and Power in a simple and easy to use kit.

Simple, Effective, Affordable!

For more information on the Solar Powered Water Generator visit www.BAHAMASSDG.com

Green SOLUTIONS

LED Lighting

Go Green with a simple switch to LED Lighting!

Imagine running your entire home or office lighting using LED Bulbs that operate on less than the equivalent power consumption of two (2) 100 watt light bulbs. With LED Lighting you can enjoy the savings of as much as 70% when compared to CFL Bulbs. Here's a rundown of the LED Advantage.

- Lower Energy: Uses 70% less energy than CFL of Equal Light Intensity.
- Directional light Emission: Directing light where it's needed.
- Size Advantage: Can be very compact and low-profile.
- Shatter Resistance: No breakable glass or filaments.
- No Harmful Mercury (HG) - No Disposal Hazard
- Instant On – Require No "warm up" time
- Rapid Cycling Capability: Lifetime not affected by frequent switching.
- Controllability: Works with electronic controls to change light levels.
- No IR or UV Emissions: Lighting LEDs do not emit IR or UV radiation.
- Lower Maintenance Costs: No Costly Ballasts or Starters to replace.
- Longer Useful Life: Avg. Range above 50,000 Hours+ (5.7 Years+)

www.OFFGRIDLED.com

Eco-Housing

Bachelor's Estates – Cat Island, Bahamas

Internationally, the construction of energy efficient housing and the integration of "green" building concepts have become more commonplace. The use of renewable energy as a viable alternative to traditional energy sources is not only efficient but affordable as well. As the cost of Solar panels and equipment has lowered over the years, the implementation of solar power generation, heat pump water heating, solar HVAC and LED lighting for residential uses has increased.

A working example of one such eco-housing concept can be found along the turquoise waters of The Bahamas, on Cat Island. Bachelor's Estates, is a beautiful stretch of land encompassing thousands of acres with palm trees, white sandy beaches, fruit trees and lush native flowers and plants.

With excellent southern exposure the site is expected to become a unique energy efficient Beachfront Bed & Breakfast venue offering all the amenities and peaceful environment "island life" signifies. The proposed wind and solar power system will meet a majority of the energy needs of each unit. Heat Pump Water Heating, Solar Air Conditioning, LED Lighting, Atmospheric Water Generation and ProTec Concrete Wall System creates an energy efficient environment that is good for the environment and promotes conservation of resources. For more information call 760-218-0518.

Check Out **BAHAMASTYLE** on   for more Information.

www.ingramcontent.com/pod-product-compliance
Lightning Source LLC
Chambersburg PA
CBHW042020150426
43197CB00002B/82